I0073684

10 Canine Tips

Real Estate
from a Dog's Point of View

*"For me a house or
an apartment
becomes a home
when you add
one set of four legs,
a happy tail,
and that indescribable
measure of love
that we call a dog."*

~Roger Caras

What's Everyone Howling About?

"Pawsitively helpful tips. A doggone must read!"

~Dan & Marcia Princinsky & Nicky

"Whether you are a buyer, seller or agent, real estate transactions can seem daunting. Jamie's book has plenty of useful tips packed into a fun and easy-to-read format. Sit, stay, and bite into great advice offered by a true professional."

~Donnita Parker

"I read Jamie's book of tips at a time when I needed it most: when I was in the process of buying a home and finding a REALTOR® that I could intuitively trust and build a good working relationship with. Jamie's tips are superb and have helped me put my recent experience and emotions into words. This is a very encouraging book to read for anyone who is planning to embark on the journey of buying or selling a home."

~Dr. Wendy Nickerson

"Jamie keeps it simple. It was a pleasure working with her to purchase our home. If you follow her guidance, you will find joy in whatever you choose to do. This is essential reading for achieving peace, prosperity, and success."

~Hugh Smith & Carole Horita

"Thanks to her unique approach to real estate, Jamie helped my daughter and I realize how important it was to feel at "Home" again. My trust in her real estate knowledge, positive attitude, and sincerity made for a smooth and stress-free transition and created a lifelong friendship in the process."

~Betty McDougal

10 Canine Tips

Real Estate from a Dog's Point of View

Copyright 2018, All Rights Reserved
Jamie and Bill Wagner

ISBN 13: 978-0-9840585-3-2

E-mail: Info@TuckerTaleProductions.com

Without limiting the rights under copyright reserved above, no part of this publication may be reproduced, stored in or introduced into a retrieval system, or transmitted, in any form, or by any means (electronic, mechanical, photocopying, recording, or otherwise), without the prior written permission of both the copyright owner and the publisher of this book.

Publishers Note: The scanning, uploading, and distribution of this book via the Internet or via any other means without the permission of the publisher is illegal. Your support of the author's rights is appreciated.

Tucker Tale Productions, Publisher

Printed in the United States of America

DEDICATION

This book is dedicated to all the canine spirits whose
inspiration and guiding light helped me pave the way to an intimate
understanding of unconditional love, loyalty, and service to others.

*To my two loving and devoted Pembroke Welsh Corgis, Taylor and Little Cooper.
Their intuitive manner and genuine love of life has been instrumental in
helping me keep my personal everyday perspective fresh, fun, and unassuming.*

*To Tyler, my little rescued stray who taught me the value of trust, tenacity,
and focus. He has always helped me follow my dreams.*

*To Shana, Sherman, Jasmine, and Bauser — four beautiful Lhasa Apsos
whose loving presence and unrelenting dedication made the trials
and tribulations of everyday life seem insignificant.*

*And finally to Tucker, my bright-eyed red
and white Corgi Son, without whom
I may never have known the meaning and
heartfelt appreciation of finally
"Coming Home!"*

*"It's not **where** you come home to
as much as it's **who** you come home to!"*

~Jamie Wagner

10 Canine Tips
Real Estate
from a Dog's Point of View

CONTENTS

*"My goal in life is
to be as good of a person
my dogs already
think I am."*

~Author Unknown

AN EARLY BEGINNING

I'm often asked, how did I begin my career and why real estate?

A long story short . . . I was four years old when my parents decided to move our family. Some families move across town, or to another city or state, but my family bought the house right next door. To this day, I can still remember carrying my favorite stuffed animal dogs to my new home just a few steps away.

The family my parents bought the house from had decided to move to a much larger property across town, and once they were settled in, they invited our family to visit their new, big, beautiful home. To me, it seemed like a castle! The old neighbor "just happened" to be a local Real Estate Broker and though I didn't know it at the time, after standing in his luxurious living room as a little girl, my life's path had been set.

Coincidently a few years later as a 4th grader my class assignment was to write a paper on someone I admired in the community. I instantly remembered our previous neighbor. I called him at his office and he granted me a formal interview for my school project. Although today I don't recall the exact questions I asked, I do know he made such an impression on me, I knew in my heart that one day I would not only live in a beautiful home myself but would eventually help others do the same.

How time flies! It's interesting how childhood events and perceptions can impact our lives as adults. To this day, I'm convinced things were set into motion by that little four-year-old girl who once stood in the middle of a bigger than life home.

The rest is history!

Jamie

P.S. I truly hope you enjoy reading this book as much as I loved creating it for you.

"Home is where your heart is,
even if you can't quite
remember which suitcase
you packed it in."

~Jamie Wagner

INTRODUCTION
GOING HOME!

10 Canine Tips
Real Estate from a Dog's Point of View

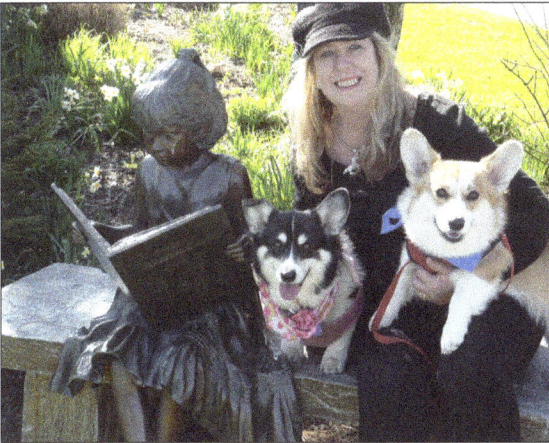

I have two adorable Pembroke Welsh Corgis, and although they may not necessarily think in the same manner as their human counterparts, they nonetheless seem to have a laser-like focus when it comes to knowing what they truly want.

Over the years, as a real estate professional, I have also had the good fortune to look beyond the obvious and realize that when it comes to residential real estate, it isn't just the acquisition or selling of a home, so much as it's developing relationships and helping others determine what their needs and wants are. It's all about creating new beginnings and the joy and contentment of finding just the right place to call "home."

The bottom line is that whether you're buying, selling, or facilitating, it's not only important to net the best possible return in the shortest period of time with the least amount of stress, but to also consider your true feelings and heartfelt objectives—the "why" of the deal, if you will. So, in keeping with the spirit of this message, here are . . .

10 Canine Tips guaranteed to facilitate your journey home!

*"If your dog
doesn't like someone,
you probably
shouldn't either."*

~Author Unknown

TIP 1: Wag your tail. Trust is key.

Is someone in your corner?

When occasional bumps in the road present themselves, building rapport, developing relationships, and creating partnerships with people you feel comfortable with and trust can help avoid uncertainty and confusion. Trust comes from a working relationship that demonstrates integrity, competence, and a sincere desire to have another's best interests at heart.

Whether you're facilitating the transaction or you are the buyer or seller, make it a point to qualify, recognize and discover the motivations, specific needs, expectations, and concerns of the parties involved.

Knowing you're not alone can make all the difference!

"A reason a dog
has so many friends
is that he wags his tail
instead of his tongue."

~Author Unknown

TIP 2: Bark, howl, but don't growl! Communication is everything.

Is anyone listening?

Make no bones about it . . . properly used, technology can provide great interpersonal support, but its limitations can also result in miscommunication. Empathy, or putting yourself in someone else's shoes and really listening, is a key component in the art of communication. Effective communication establishes a connection and involves a personal, emotional process. Without the presence of body language, voice tonality, eye contact, and facial expression, misunderstandings can and do easily occur.

Remember, it's not what you say that ultimately determines how you make people feel, as much as it's the language you use, how you choose to express it, and the meaning you give it. While a phone call, text, or email may be time savers, sometimes there's no substitute for face-to-face, up-close, personal human interaction. If Taylor & Cooper could articulate the message, I'm sure they would say, "Bark less, wag more!"

A little yipping and yapping is fine, as long as we remind ourself that words alone can sometimes get in the way.

"It's not the size of your house
that makes a home . . .
It's the size of your heart!"

~Author Unknown

TIP 3: Mark your territory and do your homework.

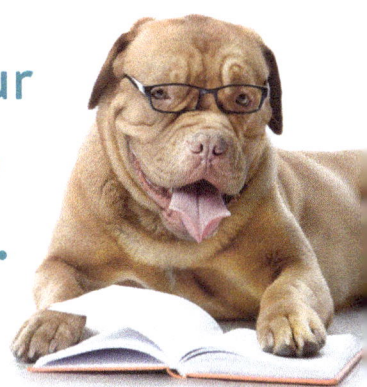

Know your market and qualify!

Get educated. Buying or selling a home can be one of the most important decisions and investments a person might make during their lifetime. Whether you're the buyer, seller, or real estate professional, researching and analyzing significant market resources will provide an essential understanding of the local marketplace and demographics to help you match a property to a specific lifestyle.

It's a process of elimination. Many factors are involved while making an informed decision, including location and surrounding neighborhoods, new construction options, inventory availability, valuation and pricing, floor plan, architectural design, features, and square footage preferences, resale flexibility, absorption and appreciation rates, local market incentives, property taxes, insurance, utility costs, HOA dues and by-laws, assessments, pre-approval and financing options, title search, closing procedures and fees, appraisals, inspections, building and home improvement costs, zoning ordinances, and identifying airports, freeways, medical facilities, neighborhood schools, parks, shopping, entertainment, and amenities. **WHEW!** But to put it simply . . .

Let your dog take you for a walk and check out the neighborhood.

*"Always put your
best paw forward!"*

~Author Unknown

TIP 4: Dive in!

Tucker makes a splash!

Take the plunge.

Test the waters in the beginning, but keep in mind, things won't start happening until you've decided you're all in. Once you've committed to your vision, it's time to take that leap of faith and move forward with a can-do attitude. Deciding and knowing what you really want and going out of your way to understand what motivates the other people in the agreement is vital.

Regardless of which end of a transaction you find yourself, there's a greater opportunity for a winning outcome when everyone's needs are acknowledged and respected.

You have a better chance of getting what you want by diving in and helping others swim after that all-important "why."

"A dog smiles with its
whole face—ears, eyes, nose,
whiskers, mouth, tongue"

~Pam Brown

TIP 5: Show your teeth. Say what you mean, and mean what you say.

A smile goes a long way.

When showing those pearly whites, whoever you're working with should see a smile backed with sincerity, respect, and a willingness to seek out amicable solutions to all issues. The importance of responding vs. reacting cannot be overstated. Facial expressions and body language that exhibit unnecessary concern, frustration, and drama can only adversely affect others' behavior.

Keep in mind, not unlike our canine friends, we can all get an intuitive vibrational sense regarding positive energy versus deception, intended or otherwise.

Elicit clarity by creating an environment of mutual trust, and avoid sending messages that can cause double-binds by saying one thing while thinking or doing the opposite. Do what you say and follow through!

Always keep your objectives in sight, but don't bite.

"Sometimes you've
got to dig a little deeper."

~Author Unknown

TIP 6: Keep on digging. Be persistent.

Move into action and never give up.

If you're a seller, there's a buyer out there for your property somewhere. And if you're a buyer, that special new home is just waiting to find you. On the other hand, should you happen to be the professional in the transaction, exhibit a "can do," persistent, positive attitude supported by an air of confident assurance and a willingness to provide great customer service.

Continue to maintain an open mind, ask lots of questions, be resourceful and determined. Keep on digging, have patience, demonstrate courage, and everyone will ultimately uncover the desired result.

Extend a paw with a serving attitude and watch others wag their tail in appreciation.

"No bones about it . . .
they see what we don't"

~Jamie Wagner

TIP 7: Keep an eye on the ball. Details! Details! Details!

Stay focused.

Maintain momentum by knowing the process, monitoring the sale, and stay alert for any potential unforeseen circumstances.

Most people expect and appreciate clear, concise, updated information, including regular feedback, marketing strategy progress, and marketplace update reports.

Keep in touch! The best possible scenario is realized when all the parties involved are personally committed to returning phone calls, answering emails in a timely fashion, staying on top of deadlines, and continue to make themselves available. In other words, dot those i's and cross those t's along the way and be sure to take a little extra time to review, understand, and document all important details. Follow up, follow up, follow up!

Keep the ball rolling.

"A dog **nose**
what feels good"

~Jamie Wagner

TIP 8: Sniff it out.
Follow your instincts.

Listen to your intuition.

If it feels right, it probably is.

But if you're not comfortable with the overall terms of the agreement, the property itself, or maybe even with the parties involved, chances are you won't be content down the road. It's much easier and less stressful to bow out early and start over than it is to try to gain confidence later. Don't become so emotionally attached to the result that you're not willing to walk away. Separate yourself from the "what" if it doesn't support your "why."

If it doesn't smell right, it probably isn't.

If too many fleas are biting, shake them off and move on.

*"Sometimes a willingness
to stand in someone else's boots
and a little devotion
to a common goal can
make all the difference"*

~Bill Wagner

TIP 9: Don't follow the pack. It's about innovation and loyalty.

Think out of the box.

In a competitive marketplace, it's essential that an agent comes to the table with specialized knowledge and an innovative marketing plan with ideas to get the word out, and it's also important that the buyer and seller show up with a demonstrated sense of loyalty.

If you're the client, it's invaluable to have a professional to confer with. It's the agent's responsibility to prepare a comparative market analysis (CMA), price the property right, offer a first impression checklist, as well as implementing dynamic, unique, and continuous marketing strategies tailored to the client's needs.

Conversely, if you happen to be a buyer or seller, resist following the pack and the impulse to switch representation when things don't appear to be moving as quickly as anticipated.

Innovation from the real estate pro and loyalty from the client produce mutually beneficial results for all.

Keep the creative collar loose and unrestricted, but never let go of the leash.

"If you think dogs can't count, try putting three dog biscuits in your pocket and giving Fido only two of them"

~Phil Pastoret

TIP 10: Sit, stay, but don't roll over. Know the process and negotiate.

It's all about perspective.

Because the various parties in a transaction view it from different vantage points, often with differing objectives, the negotiation process can appear adversarial. When working with several personalities in any transaction, collaboration as opposed to confrontation is essential.

Sometimes a little creativity while structuring the terms of the sale, knowing your bottom line, not making assumptions, being patient, and expressing sincerity is all it takes to establish an environment for fair, impartial, and effective negotiations. If all parties strive for a win-win agreement, the collective objective of closing the sale has a much better chance of becoming a reality.

Don't be afraid to chew on that bone for a while before you decide to bury it.

*"Happiness starts
with a wet nose
and ends with
a wagging tail."*

~Author Unknown

BONUS TIP: Stick your head out the window and enjoy the ride home!

Value the journey.

Whether you're the real estate expert with the task of bringing a buyer and seller together, the person looking for a place to call home, or just selling and moving on, the process can be emotional, challenging, stressful, frustrating, and can sometimes even feel overwhelming.

But with a little homework, a dash of patience, a tail waggin' attitude, and a whole lot of identifying "what" you really want and "why" you want it, there's no reason you can't— not unlike my dogs, Little Cooper and Taylor—stick your head out the window and enjoy the ride HOME!

HOME ™

*"A house is made
of bricks and beams.
A home is made
of hopes and dreams!"*

~Author Unknown

A House + Love = Home

*"A wagging tail, a friendly woof
bring joy to all beneath this roof."*

~Author Unknown

Let's Get It Sold!

A SELLER'S GUIDE FOR MARKET PREPARATION, BROKER TOURS AND OPEN HOUSES

It's About First Impressions to Secure the Best Price.

Create an experience that will engage the five senses.
What makes a buyer's eyes light up when seeing your home?

Start with Curb Appeal and a Welcoming Exterior!

🐾 **Does the front door say, "Welcome?"** Opening the front door to a home is like opening the cover of a new book. Clean, paint or varnish the door, replace any outdated hardware, doorbell, and lighting fixtures.

🐾 **Welcome Home.** Buy an attractive front door welcome mat and clean or recondition the mailbox.

🐾 **Create an inviting environment.** Place bright, colorful flowers in pots near entryways and hang a few lush plants; clean and reposition outdoor furniture.

🐾 **Make it a real showplace.** Maintain a fresh cut lawn, trim bushes, hedges, and branches; edge, rake, and add fresh mulch to flower beds. Create an inviting, clean, clear sparkling pool and spa area and open those backyard umbrellas. Watch where you walk—don't forget to clean up after the pooch!

🐾 **A debris-free and clean home inside and out creates the impression of a maintenance-free home in the mind of a potential buyer.** Sweep porches, entryway, steps, patios, balconies, pool deck, and driveway; clean exterior windows, screens, rain gutters, and brush those cobwebs and bugs away.

🐾 **It's the simple things.** Do the address house numbers have curb appeal? To enhance them, paint or buy new ones.

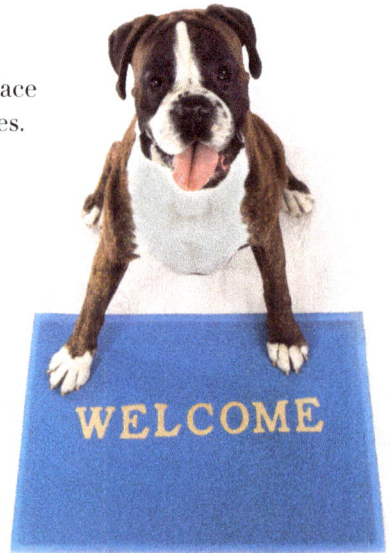

🐾 Eliminate unnecessary items from a buyer's repair checklist. Inspect and fix any drainage or structural issues; repair roof leaks, sprinkler system, septic and well systems, fences, and wash or paint garage door and exterior of home, if needed. Get replacement cost estimates for major items and insure you are in compliance with local building codes.

Come on in . . . Inspect Room by Room!

🐾 Make your home shine from top to bottom. Thoroughly clean the entire home and consider a professional cleaning service. Give special attention to the kitchen, clean appliances, floors, steam clean or replace the carpet, clean out the fireplace and sweep the chimney. Make the windows and mirrors sparkle.

🐾 Less is always more. Start packing, rearrange furniture and accessories. Add a special touch by displaying your best place setting for guests at the dining room table. Eliminate clutter and remove excess furniture, nick nacks, small counter kitchen appliances, refrigerator magnets, bathroom toothbrushes, perfumes, magazines, toys, and pet items. What? Hide the puppy toys?

🐾 Create a generic and comfortable environment. Depersonalize each room and put away family photos, teenage posters, and personal collections, including artwork. Remove any attached items that are not included in the sale or tag them with "to be replaced" or "not included" in the sale, such as a special chandelier, entertainment center, or mirror.

🐾 Tidy up. Make the beds, organize closets, drawers, cabinets, pantry, garage and attic; buyers might just peek.

🐾 Fresh is better. Replace or buy new towels in bathrooms, install new shower curtain, freshen bedroom linen, and clean draperies; also put those toilet seats down and give the dog a bath.

🐾 Engage the sense. Add a touch of an appealing light fresh scent; simmer a few drops of vanilla, orange or lemon peels on the stove, or bake cookies to serve to guests; refrain from smoking and be sensitive to pet odors. Really! What pet odors?

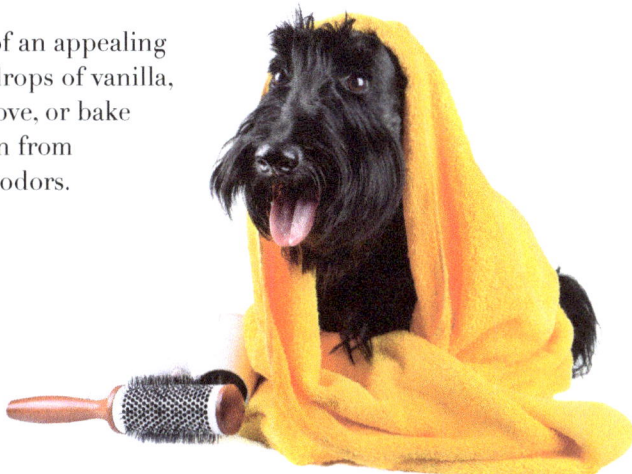

🐾 For optimum effect. Place fresh flowers and indoor plants in strategic locations; display a fresh bowl of fruit in kitchen.

🐾 Bring the outside in. Open curtains, shades, and blinds to showcase nice views; turn on lights, lamps, and fans to accent; open doors between rooms.

🐾 Create a mood. It's not what they think, it's what they feel. Play soft music, turn off TV, computers, video games, and other electronics, and turn on soothing indoor or outdoor water fountains, and light the cozy gas fireplace.

🐾 No surprises. Pre-inspect and make any necessary repairs to air conditioning/heating units, plumbing, electrical, major appliances, security system, attic, etc.; replace or clean filters; assemble all warranties and manuals.

🐾 Attention to detail. Use touch-up paint on walls or paint any room with neutral colors if necessary, caulk or spackle where needed, fix dripping faucets and showerheads, patch holes in walls, and replace light bulbs; check for operation of smoke and carbon monoxide detectors.

🐾 Should You or Shouldn't You? Do your homework before investing in major home improvements. Consider cost vs. value, the local market, and competition. Maybe a home staging expert might help make your home more appealing.

🐾 Secure your valuables. Place all money, jewelry, prescriptions, medications, and personal documents in a secure place.

🐾 Every showing counts. Be flexible to take advantage of every opportunity to show your home.

🐾 And finally, give the family a day off! Plan an activity and get away. Enjoy the day away from home with the kids and pets during a showing or open house event!

Movin' on Down the Road

A BUYER AND SELLER'S MOVING CHECKLIST

You've decided to move-on . . . so let's go home!

☐ Locate reputable moving companies to secure estimates. Compare costs, terms, and insurance rates. Get the agreement in writing and read it carefully. The day and month of the actual move may determine final fees. Is an auto transport company, rental truck, cargo trailer, or a storage facility required?

☐ Get organized. Create a special folder for moving documents and keep receipts for tax deductions.

☐ Sort and sell. Plan a garage sale to eliminate stuff to pack and gain some extra cash.

☐ Locate a charity. Donate and schedule a pick-up. Leave the old and start new!

☐ Dispose. Eliminate propane tanks, paint, mower gasoline, and toxins.

☐ Secure packing supplies. Obtain various size boxes, bubble wrap, tape, padding, and markers.

☐ Take inventory of belongings. Create a handwritten list, photographs, or video.

☐ Gather up papers. Assemble home warranties, instruction booklets, extra keys, etc.

☐ Get the kids involved. Provide moving assignments for everyone.

☐ Start packing. Label boxes based on room location and mark fragile on designated boxes.

☐ Declutter and clean room by room. It's never too early to start cleaning house.

☐ Change of address reminders. Notify friends and family, banks, credit cards, insurance companies including: auto, home, life, property, medical, and RV; taxes, voter's registration, driver's license and vehicle tags, social security, magazine or newspaper subscriptions, memberships, professional licenses, phone, electric, cable, internet, websites, security system, and home warranty. The list goes on . . . professional services: doctors, vet and pet ID chip company, lawn and pool care, handyman, cleaning service, plumber, electrician, pest control, mechanic, accountant, attorney, hairdresser, transfer prescriptions, and any final billings, etc.

- [ ] **Arrange dates to disconnect and reconnect.** Contact phone, cable, internet, electric, water, trash, security system, gas services, pool, lawn, cleaning services, and pest control, etc.

- [ ] **Time off.** Coordinate the necessary dates with business obligations, employers, and schools.

- [ ] **Pack and move your own personal small valuables.** Place prescriptions, jewelry, important documents: passports, banking, insurance, computer files, will, and birth certificates in a separate box for safe keeping on moving day.

- [ ] **Pick-up and deliver.** Visit dry cleaners, return any borrowed items, i.e. library books.

- [ ] **Transport plants or flowers.** Plan a safe arrival based on potential temperature change.

- [ ] **Children's school records.** Transfer records and register at the new school.

- [ ] **Medical records.** Secure any medical records and reports prior to moving out of area.

- [ ] **White glove cleaning.** Schedule a cleaning company to do one final clean.

- [ ] **Discover your new neighborhood.** Get involved prior to moving and locate new professional service providers, grocery stores, post office, restaurants, entertainment, community activities, and area amenities.

- [ ] **Meet your new neighbors.** Stop by and say "hi," and start making new friends.

- [ ] **Saying good bye.** Allow time to schedule visits with existing friends and neighbors.

- [ ] **Design and sketch.** Place your furniture placement on paper in advance for delivery and prepare for new window treatment, if needed.

- [ ] **Change locks.** Find a locksmith and schedule an appointment at your new home.

☐ Prepare a "must have box." Prior to moving, assemble a separate box for moving day. Add some cash, water, snacks, any necessary medical supplies, TP, paper towels, cleaning products, bath towels and soap, pens, paper, trash bags, scissors, tape, tools, flashlight, cell phone charger, tooth brush and paste, maps, jackets, blankets and linens, etc.

☐ Moving with small children. On moving day, secure a sitter and provide the kids with books, games, crafts, and snacks to keep them busy and safe.

☐ Moving with pets. Taylor and Cooper have a few words to share . . . Don't forget to pack the pooch.

Prior to moving! Update pup shots, find a new vet, make new identification collar tags, and schedule a date to contact the chip ID company to provide updated information. Secure your pet's medical records to transfer if moving out of the area.

On moving day! Transport food, treats, chews, meds, fencing, crates, leashes, bed, and favorite toys in car. Don't forget the water and food bowls. If you're moving out of the immediate area, determine whether there are any special concerns, meds, or vaccines that may be required in the new environment. Consider a pet sitter or designate a safe location to prevent any accidents or injuries during a busy moving day.

☐ Plan your work and work your plan!

"I've traveled far,
from East to West
searching for a home,
sat with friends
in crowded rooms
feeling so alone,
always moving forward
running from the past,
till one day a little bird told
the truth at last . . .
. . . Home is where the Heart is.
This was my journey!"

~Author Unknown

HOMEWORK NOTES

For Planning Your Move

Our Moving
To-Do List

"Home is creating the
conditions from which
your purpose
can find you."

~Author Unknown

"May your home know joy,
every room hold laughter and
every window open to great possibilities!"

~Maryanne Radmacher-Hershey

MEET THE AUTHORS

Whether you're moving across town, across country, or just moving on, as a successful real estate professional, **Jamie Wagner** thinks out of the box and understands the stress and uncertainty associated during any real estate transition. In addition, her background as a personal lifestyle coach combined with the loving respect for her intuitive canine kids provides Jamie with a unique insight into the motivations and emotional perceptions of buyers, sellers, and fellow real estate agents. She realizes that the obvious "what" tends to obscure the all-important "why," and how discovering the psychology behind a home sale can make all the difference in terms of a rewarding outcome for all parties involved.

Jamie is passionate about inspiring and helping others "move on" to new beginnings. She conducts inspirational presentations and workshops, provides one-on-one personal coaching and consulting services, and pursues her love of the literary arts. Jamie has chalked up thousands of miles touring the country in the family RV. She feels most at home cooking and entertaining friends and family with her husband Bill and her two loving Pembroke Welsh Corgis, Taylor and Little Cooper, who never fail to accept life's treats with gratitude.

Wishing you a home filled with Love, Contentment, & Joy,

Jamie ❤

*"Whoever said that diamonds are
a girl's best friend . . . never had a dog."*

~Author Unknown

MY LITERARY TEAM

Taylor Louise, Co-Author

Little Cooper, Co-Author

Hi there! We are two loving Pembroke Welsh Corgis, and underneath all our fur we're full of unconditional love and enjoy touching the hearts of people we meet every day. We have fun romping outdoors, playing with friends, squeaking our favorite toys, floating in the swimming pool, and visiting shops and restaurants everywhere during our travels and adventures.

But most of all, we have found that the simple pleasures of life like drinking a bowl of ice cold water, savoring tasty treats, experiencing belly rubs, bringing smiles to others, and just appreciating the time we spend playing ball and cuddling with our mom and dad at home is the best part of all.

We love getting out of the house to scratch, sniff, and explore, but it's always good to come back home again!

Licks & Kisses, XXOO

Taylor & Cooper

A Special Thank You

A special thanks to our dear friend and literary analyst extraordinaire, David Robert Ord, who graciously provided his expertise and professional editorial services to the success of our work. Also, many thanks to Susan Malikowski of Designleaf Studio who intuitively shared my vision and turned the cover and interior design into a reality for *10 Canine Tips*.

*"In a perfect world,
every dog would have a home
and every home would have a dog."*

~Author Unknown

A SPECIAL MESSAGE FROM TAYLOR & COOPER

Are you thinking about bringing a four-legged friend home?

If you should decide to enjoy all the benefits of animal companionship and an unconditional loving relationship with a new canine friend, Cooper and I have a few "extra tips."

When selecting your best friend, look for a breed that might be compatible with your family's environment and lifestyle. Prior to introducing a new pet, we invite you to thoroughly research reputable rescue organizations, kennels, adoption resources, breeders, and shelters. Or, you might consider fostering, volunteering, or donating to a special organization to help our four-legged friends find their way home.

Remember, the best part of the day is coming home to a wagging tail!

More Licks and Kisses, XXOO

Taylor Louise & Little Cooper

"Dogs are like potato chips . . .
you can't have just one!"

~Author Unknown

Come One, Come All!

Join Jamie for an educational, inspirational, and entertaining presentation or workshop event based on one of her books.

Purchase your copy of *10 Canine Tips* at:
Amazon.com or BarnesandNoble.com

For more information on presentations, workshop events, success training, or personal and professional coaching and consulting:

Email *Jamie@10RealEstateTips.com*

or Visit *www.10RealEstateTips.com*

Inquire about bulk purchases or group discounts for *10 Canine Tips* or any other Tucker Tale Productions Titles at

Info@TuckerTaleProductions.com

DON'T MISS OTHER BOOKS
BY JAMIE AND BILL WAGNER

Also Available as a Companion to *10 Canine Tips: Real Estate from a Dog's Point of View*

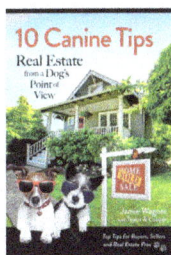

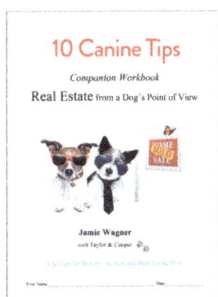

10 Canine Tips: Companion Workbook—A great interactive tool filled with strategies, questions, additional tips, and action exercises designed to provide practical guidance and successful results for Buyers, Sellers, and Real Estate Professionals.

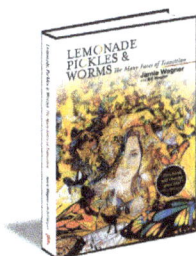

Lemonade, Pickles & Worms: The Many Faces of Transition—an adult personal development, transformational guide designed to help people from all walks of life move-on when the way we have lived our life isn't working anymore. Learn how to turn the sour lemons of life into sweet lemonade.

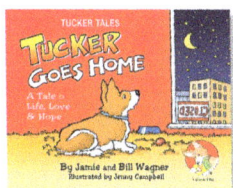

Tucker Goes Home: A Tale of Life, Love & Hope—the first value based children's book in The Tucker Tales Collection sets the stage for a lifetime of adventures for Tucker, a curious, mischievous, and lovable Pembroke Welch Corgi puppy. Follow Tucker's journey as he longs for a sense of belonging and the security of a new home and family. Watch as he overcomes worry, uncertainty, and fear by gradually learning and applying the positive values of love, courage, and compassion.

Through Their Eyes: Seeing What They See—a collection of canine parables designed to give us all a unique perspective on this cherished gift we call life. View the world through the eyes of our canine friends and see how intuitive and totally in sync they seem to be with the perpetual laws that govern the universe and how their behavior appears to mirror that of the most enlightened sage.

"Every ending is a new beginning."

Home is where your story begins!

www.ingramcontent.com/pod-product-compliance
Lightning Source LLC
Chambersburg PA
CBHW040154200326
41521CB00019B/2606